N Y   W H I T E

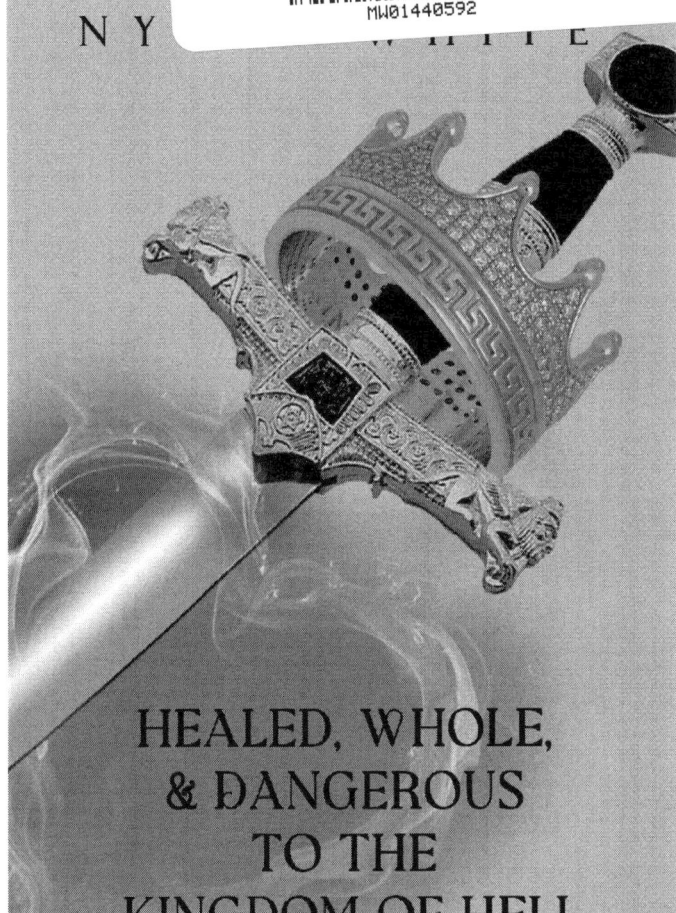

HEALED, WHOLE, & DANGEROUS TO THE KINGDOM OF HELL

Copyright © 2023 by Nykia White
Healed, Whole, and Dangerous to the Kingdom of Hell

All Rights Reserved. No part of this book may be used or reproduced by any means, graphic, electronic, or mechanical, including photocopying, recording, taping, or by any information storage retrieval system without the written permission of the publisher except in the case of brief quotations embodied in critical articles and reviews.

Purposeful Scents, LLC
Assisted by Scribe Empire, LLC
Cover design by: Angela Mills Camper of Dezign Pro Printing & Graphics

THE HOLY BIBLE, NEW INTERNATIONAL VERSION®, NIV® Copyright © 1973, 1978, 1984, 2011 by Biblica, Inc

Holy Bible, New Living Translation, copyright © 1996, 2004, 2015 by Tyndale House Foundation. "Official King James Bible Online." King James Bible Online, https://www.kingjamesbibleonline.org/.

The Holy Bible: Amplified Version. Zondervan Pub. House, 1987.

Scripture quotations marked MSG are taken from THE MESSAGE, copyright © 1993, 2002, 2018 by Eugene H. Peterson.
Printed in the United States of America
First Printing, 2023

ISBN:979-8-9887983-0-9

Disclaimer: The information presented in this book is based on my personal experiences. I am not a mental health professional.

DEDICATION

I dedicate this book to those the Enemy has deceived and made to feel as if they have to live with trauma, brokenness, and torment, ultimately leaving them to think that death is the only option to relieve the pain.

You are more precious than rubies, and the sufferings of your present time are not worthy to be compared to the glory that shall be revealed in you!

I pray this book encourages you to go deeper in healing and wholeness.

TABLE OF CONTENTS

Dedication

Testimonials 9

Introduction – The Well Experience 11

Chapter 1 – Wounded from the Beginning 21

Chapter 2 – Open Wounds 29

Chapter 3 – The One Who Restores 39

Chapter 4 – Transformation 49

Chapter 5 – Freedom 55

Affirmations of Identity in Christ 68

Exercises 74

Prayers 84

Resources 93

Bibliography 95

About the Author 97

TESTIMONIALS

*T*his book allowed me to do a lot of self-reflection on my healing journey and where I was in my walk with Christ. The transparency of the author, along with the exercises and affirmations reminded me not only of who I am but how dangerous I am as a healed vessel of God!

Keante Jacobs

This book contains very transparent and needed truth. The exercises are great, practical things for readers to do. The prayers are powerful, and the affirmations empower and encourage the readers. I believe this book will help many people!

Khatarrie Durden

Nykia opens her book with the woman at the well. She explains the beauty and healing that Jesus brings to those who have been wounded. Jesus truly sees us. She gives you insight into her personal

Testimonials

experience of being wounded emotionally and how God is taking her through a process of healing to make her whole. The things she faced were painful but with God, we can and shall overcome and defeat the Enemy.

I loved everything about this book. As believers, we need to face the truth about our past pain, so we can move forward to wholeness without trauma holding us back. The blessings of the Lord make us rich and add no sorrow. This book also has guided prayers that will encourage you as you walk this journey out.

Adriana Simmons

INTRODUCTION

THE WELL EXPERIENCE

Jesus realized that the Pharisees were keeping count of the baptisms that he and John performed (although his disciples, not Jesus, did the actual baptizing). They had posted the score that Jesus was ahead, turning him and John into rivals in the eyes of the people. So Jesus left the Judean countryside and went back to Galilee.

To get there, he had to pass through Samaria. He came into Sychar, a Samaritan village that bordered the field Jacob had given his son Joseph. Jacob's well was still there. Jesus, worn out by the trip, sat down at the well. It was noon.

Introduction

A woman, a Samaritan, came to draw water. Jesus said, "Would you give me a drink of water?" (His disciples had gone to the village to buy food for lunch.)

The Samaritan woman, taken aback, asked, "How come you, a Jew, are asking me, a Samaritan woman, for a drink?" (Jews in those days wouldn't be caught dead talking to Samaritans.)

Jesus answered, "If you knew the generosity of God and who I am, you would be asking me for a drink, and I would give you fresh, living water."

The woman said, "Sir, you don't even have a bucket to draw with, and this well is deep. So how are you going to get this 'living water'? Are you a better man than our ancestor Jacob, who dug this well and drank from it, he and his sons and livestock, and passed it down to us?"

Jesus said, "Everyone who drinks this water will get thirsty again and again. Anyone who drinks the water I give will never thirst—not ever. The water I give will be an artesian spring within, gushing fountains of endless life."

The woman said, "Sir, give me this water so I won't ever get thirsty, won't ever have to come back to this well again!"

He said, "Go call your husband and then come back."

"I have no husband," she said.
"That's nicely put: 'I have no husband.' You've had five husbands, and the man you're living with now isn't even your husband. You spoke the truth there, sure enough."

"Oh, so you're a prophet! Well, tell me this: Our ancestors worshiped God at this mountain, but you Jews insist that Jerusalem is the only place for worship, right?"

"Believe me, woman, the time is coming when you Samaritans will worship the father neither here at this mountain nor there in Jerusalem. You worship guessing in the dark; we

Introduction

Jews worship in the clear light of day. God's way of salvation is made available through the Jews. But the time is coming—it has, in fact, come—when what you're called will not matter and where you go to worship will not matter.

"It's who you are and the way you live that count before God. Your worship must engage your spirit in the pursuit of truth. That's the kind of people the Father is out looking for: those who are simply and honestly themselves before him in their worship. God is sheer being itself—Spirit. Those who worship him must do it out of their very being, their spirits, their true selves, in adoration."

The woman said, "I don't know about that. I do know that the Messiah is coming. When he arrives, we'll get the whole story."

"I am he," said Jesus. "You don't have to wait any longer or look any further."

Just then his disciples came back. They were shocked. They couldn't believe he was talking with that kind of a woman. No one said what they were all thinking, but their faces showed it.

The woman took the hint and left. In her confusion she left her water pot. Back in the village she told the people, "Come see a man who knew all about the things I did, who knows me inside and out. Do you think this could be the Messiah?" And they went out to see for themselves.

In the meantime, the disciples pressed him, "Rabbi, eat. Aren't you going to eat?"

He told them, "I have food to eat you know nothing about."

The disciples were puzzled. "Who could have brought him food?"

Jesus said, "The food that keeps me going is that I do the will of the One who sent me, finishing the work he started. As you look around right now, wouldn't you say that in about four months it will be time to harvest?

Introduction

Well, I'm telling you to open your eyes and take a good look at what's right in front of you. These Samaritan fields are ripe. It's harvest time!

"The Harvester isn't waiting. He's taking his pay, gathering in this grain that's ripe for eternal life. Now the Sower is arm in arm with the Harvester, triumphant. That's the truth of the saying, 'This one sows, that one harvests.' I sent you to harvest a field you never worked. Without lifting a finger, you have walked in on a field worked long and hard by others."

Many of the Samaritans from that village committed themselves to him because of the woman's witness: "He knew all about the things I did. He knows me inside and out!" They asked him to stay on, so Jesus stayed two days. A lot more people entrusted their lives to him when they heard what he had to say. They said to the woman, "We're no longer taking this on your say-so. We've heard it for ourselves and know it for sure. He's the Savior of the world!" (John 4:1-42 The Message)

*T*he Samaritan woman questioned Jesus because she didn't fully understand His ability to meet us where we are, regardless of gender, race, or social status. Even in her sinful state, Jesus offered His love and mercy to her. God accepts all, no matter what you have done or been through. It's never too late to repent and get right with God.

Second, God knows our sins and shortcomings and wants to reveal Himself as a Savior, Redeemer, and Healer who can grant us eternal life.

Third, the Samaritan woman exemplifies the importance of sharing our testimony with others. When she believed, she eagerly ran off to tell others. Her words had a profound impact, as Scripture states, "Many Samaritans from the village believed in him because of the woman's testimony, 'he told me everything I ever did'" (John 4:39 NIV). Your testimony is a powerful tool for sharing faith.

Lastly, the Samaritan woman's testimony illustrates how a single encounter with Jesus can forever change one's life. Through a simple conversation, she was healed.

Like the Samaritan woman, I have felt rejected and inadequate. I have also been filled with shame and embarrassment due to various experiences and actions. I constantly found myself attempting to fill an unfillable void. I was hurting, but I tried to cover the pain with temporary satisfactions like sex, drinking, and toxic relationships. I longed for the everlasting satisfaction of the living water from a well that would never run dry. It wasn't until I had my personal "Well" experience that I realized I needed to stop seeking answers outside of God. Living a life filled with pain is not God's desire for us. You don't have to mask the pain and suffer in silence. God is a healer. He longs to heal our wounds and take away our pain and hurt.

Emotional wounds are often overlooked because they are internal and not visible to the naked eye. These wounds may lie dormant for a while, but when triggered, they reveal what's inside of us. As believers, we shouldn't seek to fill our voids with worldly desires; instead, we should seek the source.

You can come to the Father; He is our source. He will provide all you need in life and fulfill your desires. "And my God will liberally supply (fill to full) your every need according to his riches and glory in Christ Jesus" (Philippians 4:19 Amplified Bible). If your heart is hurting, know that God is waiting with open arms to fill your voids and bring healing. Healing is not an overnight process; it involves time and partnering with God to be healed. If we trust God with our brokenness, He will bring restoration and wholeness.

Like the Samaritan woman, I have a testimony to share. Come and read about a man who told me everything I ever did and healed my heart.

Healing doesn't happen overnight; grow through the process!

CHAPTER 1

WOUNDED FROM THE BEGINNING

We don't choose the families we are born into, control where we are born, or decide what we will look like. All of these aspects are predetermined by God, who has a divine plan for our lives, even in our mothers' wombs. However, it is important to recognize that the Enemy seeks to pervert every plan of God. Consequently, we often find ourselves in daunting and overwhelming circumstances that may leave us questioning: why me? Why did I have to go through this? Why did I have to endure such traumatic experiences at a young age?

I've asked myself these questions multiple times, and perhaps you have too. Yet, we must ponder whether it is solely about us or if it is about what God wants to accomplish in our bloodlines through us. It's a deeply stirring and thought-provoking question, isn't it?

From what I can remember, everything seemed to start okay. At a young age, I had a deep love for the Lord. I grew up in a home with nine children, and our parents raised us in church, rarely missing a Sunday. That was my introduction to God. I actively served, sang in the youth choir, praise danced, and participated in youth ministry.

I had a short prayer routine before bed, and my mother would pray over me and anoint me with oil. Though I didn't fully comprehend the significance of these actions, I knew they held importance. You understand what I'm trying to convey, right? My foundation started solid, but it felt as if the rug was suddenly pulled out from under me. Keep reading, and you will soon understand the meaning behind this statement.

Growing up, I had no recollection of generational curses or their meaning. However, I was about to encounter what was in my bloodline sooner or later.

During my upbringing, my mother primarily worked as a homemaker, and my father supported the household through his work. Due to my father's extensive work commitments, we had limited time to build a father-daughter bond. As children, we learn both positive and negative behaviors by observing and imitating our parents. I witnessed adultery, domestic violence, and arguments during my childhood. I was never shown what it means to have a healthy marriage or to receive proper love from a man. I distinctly remember thinking as a child that if this is what marriage looks like, I'm never getting married.

Around the age of ten, God started showing me things in my dreams. However, at the same time, I began battling with the spirit of fear and tormenting spirits. Whenever I lay down to sleep, I could hear the Enemy telling me that if I fell asleep, I would die in my sleep. Most nights involved me fighting against sleep. When the torment got worse, I would awaken my mother for her to pray for peace over me. As the last year of elementary school ended, the summer began. During this time, weekends were spent going to spend time with relatives.

One weekend, I spent the night at one of my relative's houses and a male family member told me to come upstairs with him. Not knowing what was about to happen, I followed him. As soon as I got upstairs, he began to touch me and have intercourse with me. He told me what to do to him, and I followed the instructions. I left that weekend, and I didn't tell anyone about what happened. A few weeks went by, and I was back over at the same relative's house. This time, two of my male family members took me to the same room and had intercourse with me.

One of my male relatives told me he was my boyfriend and that he loved me. It got to the point where I felt it was normal because it happened so often. At this early age, I was developing the mindset that sex meant a man loved you. The day the incest stopped occurring, I felt abandoned and confused. The male family members went on with their lives as if nothing had ever happened, and I was left trying to process what had been happening all that time.

After experiencing incest, this opened the door to me feeling it was okay to do what had been done to me. Soon after, I got invited to a friend's house to spend a night. That night, I tried to touch a male adult inappropriately.

My parents asked me what happened the next day and I remember lying. I told my parents I wasn't aware of what I was doing. I was afraid to tell them that I was imitating what had been done to me.

As time progressed, I learned that a female family member was also experiencing incest with the same male family member and that other family members were also being molested by each other. Still unable to process everything, I was left with a feeling of betrayal and abandonment because I believed they truly loved me.

Throughout my upbringing, I always heard the phrase "What happens in this house remains in this house," which prevented me from expressing my true emotions. I simply wanted to act as if this never happened to me. So, I made an inner vow to take these secrets to the grave with me and never disclose the incest to anyone. An inner vow is a self-directed and self-focused promise that we make to ourselves in response to difficulty, frustration, or pain. I repeatedly told myself that it was better to keep this secret quiet.

The summer passed, and it was time for me to enter middle school. During middle school, I joined the marching band and cheerleading to keep myself busy. I didn't have time to think about the voids I felt. In my last year of middle school, I met a friend who introduced me to a boy who had a crush on me. I received a note from him asking me to be his girlfriend. I told him "Yeah," and he began buying me gifts that I took home, and my parents found out I had a boyfriend. They eventually met him and allowed us to hang out since I was in high school. The peer pressure began with my peers talking about having sex, while all I could think about was what had happened to me.

I became very quiet and kept to myself. People labeled me as lame and quiet because I didn't want to do what everyone else was doing. Throughout high school, my boyfriend and I grew closer and became best friends. As we started expressing our love for each other, I found myself engaging in sex again. We began making plans to be together after high school. I was ready for the world—or so I thought.

Unhealed trauma from childhood becomes the drama in marriage.

CHAPTER 2

OPEN WOUNDS

After graduating from high school, my boyfriend and I attended Job Corps in Kentucky. A few months into our time at Job Corps, my boyfriend proposed to me. I was both excited and nervous, but I said yes. I explained to him that I was afraid of having a dysfunctional marriage, so I wanted us to take some time to grow individually before getting married.

A lot was happening in my life during that time. I was stressed and missing my family back home, which started to take a toll on my physical health. I gained weight and began experiencing depression. While at Job Corps, I had to be flown back home to St. Louis for an emergency visit with my doctor due to abnormal bleeding that had lasted for a month.

During the doctor's visit, they informed me that they believed I was experiencing a miscarriage and also diagnosed me with chlamydia. I was given antibiotics to treat the chlamydia and underwent a hysteroscopy D&C procedure to clean and examine my womb. At the time, I was eighteen years old, and the doctor told me that I would not be able to bear children.

Although I was young and not actively focused on having children at that moment, what the doctors said stayed in the back of my mind. I shared the doctor's report with my boyfriend, only to find out that he had lied about not giving me chlamydia. It turned out he had contracted it from someone else and had already received treatment before I found out. As a result, we broke up.

A year passed, and I had forgiven my ex, so we started dating again. My father wasn't happy with my decision, so I decided to move out of my parents' house and get my own place. My boyfriend moved in with me, and my lifestyle started to change rapidly. I started drinking, smoking, and doing everything I wanted to do. My boyfriend and I even got each other's names tattooed on ourselves. In my mind, I was having fun and feeling free.

When I turned twenty-two, my boyfriend proposed to me once again. In July 2015, we decided to get married at the courthouse. I chose to tell my parents the night before, and although they showed up to support me, I could tell they were angry. I remember asking my boyfriend if he was sure we were making the right decision, and he assured me that we loved each other. Little did I know that love alone is not enough to sustain a marriage.

About a year after getting married, I stopped going to church, and my whole world started to shift. I found myself being manipulated by my husband, doing whatever I could to make him happy out of fear of having a dysfunctional marriage or getting divorced. I reluctantly agreed to have threesomes with my husband and other people because he wanted to add "fun" to our marriage. I also discovered an attraction to women and started being with them when my husband wasn't around.

Months later, a woman my husband had previously dated came forward with a child that was his. Confused and depressed, I couldn't believe all of this was happening in my marriage. I believed marriage was supposed to be happy and fulfilling. Instead of addressing the issues, I turned to drinking and worked more to suppress the pain.

My husband and the mother of his child worked on co-parenting, and in his guilt, he convinced me that we should try for a child of our own. Knowing that I might face difficulties getting pregnant, we started seeing a fertility specialist. I was diagnosed with polycystic ovary syndrome (PCOS) and a blocked fallopian tube. Months went by, and I couldn't conceive naturally. I made the decision to donate my eggs to help another woman struggling with infertility and opted to try in vitro fertilization for myself.

In vitro fertilization (IVF) is a procedure in which eggs are removed from a woman's ovary and combined with sperm outside of the body to form embryos. The embryos are grown in a laboratory for several days and then placed in the woman's uterus. I started the process of IVF and had my embryos placed inside my uterus. I was placed on bed rest and given daily progesterone shots to prevent a miscarriage. I found out that the woman I donated my eggs to had become pregnant with twins. I was happy for her family but couldn't wait to find out my own results.

Weeks went by, and I remember waking up one morning and hearing God saying, "It isn't over yet." A few hours later, I received a call from my nurse stating that my blood levels had shown I had miscarried. Devastated, I broke down and began to isolate myself from everyone.

I was hurt and became bitter, questioning God. How could I miscarry while helping someone conceive at the same time? I didn't understand why nothing seemed to be working out for me. My husband ended up telling his family and some of my family that I had miscarried, and people began to speak curses over me, saying that I would never have children. I felt useless and sensed the need to prove them wrong. I took the next steps of having surgery to open my fallopian tubes and remove the cyst from my reproductive organs. The surgery went well, but my right fallopian tube remained blocked.

After recovering from surgery, I found out that my husband was cheating, and he had told other women that I couldn't have children. I felt betrayed, and we began to argue more. Physical and verbal abuse ensued in our marriage, leading to our separation. Around the same time, my parents were going through marriage problems, and they decided to get a divorce. This was tough for me because I was accustomed to spending time with my entire family. The divorce caused separation within our family during the holidays, which was another adjustment I had to get used to. It was at this moment that I realized the things I had feared as a child had become a reality in my own marriage.

My husband and I decided to seek counseling and reconciliation. I slowly returned to church and took my husband along. One Sunday, we visited a church for the first time, and the pastor began to address my husband, speaking about me being a child of God and how God wouldn't let him continue to mistreat His daughter.

In the midst of everything I was going through, I realized that I was on the heart of God. I didn't know the pastor, and nobody knew the extent of my struggles, so I knew God was speaking to us. This showed me the depth of God's forgiveness. Even during the times when I wasn't living right, God had been listening to my cries. On that same day at church, I received the gift of speaking in tongues. We attended church a few more times together until my husband decided he no longer wanted to go.

He began using the church as an excuse to manipulate me and accused me of cheating every time I left the house. As I distanced myself from the church, we started to face financial struggles. We were living paycheck to paycheck and eventually got evicted, leading us to stay with my family temporarily.

The following year, I spent most of my time working two jobs while my husband spent time going in and out of clubs. Every night he didn't come home, I was confronted with the past trauma of abandonment I had experienced as a child. I cried out to God, asking Him to fix my marriage. Things would improve for a while before getting worse again. I couldn't understand why God wasn't answering my prayers. I started to hate my husband, and I became emotionally unstable. I pleaded with him, desperately trying to make him see my worth when I couldn't see it within myself.

In the last two years of my marriage, I discovered that my husband was leading a double life, engaging in relationships with both genders. It was hard for me to see pictures and still be lied to, that's when I decided to leave for good. Even though I knew I was doing the right thing, I felt worthless. I experienced low self-esteem, and everything I was dealing with emotionally on the inside began to manifest outwardly.

Feeling unloved and rejected, I started telling myself that something had to be wrong with me. Depression, anxiety, and suicidal thoughts clouded my mind. I could hear the lies of the Enemy telling me that I had nothing to live for, and each day seemed to bring more difficulties. I recognized that my marriage and unresolved trauma had led me to this place. Even as I began to take authority over suicidal thoughts, I still felt stuck in life.

During this period of despair, I started praying again, seeking God for healing. As I sought God, I surrendered to His will for my life. I prayed, "Nevertheless not my will but thine will be done" (Luke 22:41-42 KJV). Instead of asking God to fix my marriage, I started asking Him to guide me in what to do with my marriage. God spoke clearly to me and said, "If you want faithfulness, you have to let go of unfaithfulness." After being separated from my husband for a year, in September 2019, I filed for divorce.

Not yet fully divorced, I ended up finding a man to hang out with and have sex with, trying to mask the pain. One day at work, I confided in a friend about what I was going through. My friend was honest with me and said that I was sinning and committing adultery because, even though I was separated, I was still bound by the covenant until the divorce was finalized. He asked me why I would give my body to someone and allow him into my life if he didn't serve any purpose.

At this point, I noticed I was reverting to having sex again because it made me feel loved the same way I felt as a child. I ended the sexual relationship with that man, and my friend helped me realize I needed to make a lasting change in my life. It wasn't healthy for me to keep trying to cover up the deep wounds I had. I wasn't the same person I was before I got married, and I needed God to transform me.

I finally reached a point of being fed up and desired God to heal every wound and bring positive change to my life.

Your story is a part of who you are; embrace it!

CHAPTER 3

THE ONE WHO RESTORES

On the path of changing my life, God started giving me dreams about the church I needed to attend. I went to that church and got baptized for the first time. I repented, started changing, and began to see things from a different perspective. God was opening the eyes of my understanding, and I realized I had never truly had a relationship with Him. I had only approached God when I needed something. I had merely been going through the motions of attending church because it was something my parents had raised me to do. I was stuck in religious rituals, but God revealed that He desires a genuine relationship with His sons and daughters.

This marked the beginning of my journey to develop a personal relationship with God. As I talked to people about getting a divorce, many of them quoted, "Therefore what God has joined together, let no one separate" (Mark 10:9 NIV). However, I had already heard God telling me to leave the unfaithful. I went to God again to ensure I was making the right decision. He showed me that He hadn't joined me with my ex-husband. I realized that my initial mistake was not acknowledging God in our relationship or seeking His guidance before marrying him.

God revealed to me that the marriage had been used as a demonic assignment to hinder me from walking in my God-given purpose. He showed me that I had allowed the Enemy to lure me into a connection with a man who struggled with the same familiar spirits I was battling, such as lust and perversion. This only intensified the challenges in our marriage.

Within four months of filing for divorce, the divorce was finalized in January of 2020. After the divorce, I struggled to break the ungodly soul tie between my ex-husband and me. I would reach out to him to check if he was okay, still trying to maintain a close friendship.

My ex-husband would unexpectedly show up to see how I was doing, and I would answer his calls, even when I didn't want to talk to him. It was at that time that God spoke to me and said, "Let the dead bury the dead" and urged me to sever the soul tie.

In a dream, God highlighted my tattoos, and later, I realized that because I had tattoos of my ex-husband's name and our wedding date, they were still keeping me attached to him. I began the process of having the tattoos covered. Even though we were physically divorced, the soul tie still needed to be broken. I had to let go of the images I had held in my mind about our marriage.

I broke the soul tie by going through deliverance, repenting, and divorcing it. I renounced the words I had spoken, such as "I would never leave him" and "my body belonged to him." I blocked my ex-husband's number on my phone and social media. I cut off connections with his family and people who were closely associated with him. I had to pray for God's help in forgiving both my ex-husband and myself for enduring the pain year after year.

Forgiveness became a journey for me. I started fasting because bitterness and unforgiveness were deeply rooted in my heart. I knew my husband since middle school, and every time thoughts of what he did arose, I had to turn to God and ask for assistance in forgiving. I never received a genuine apology from my ex-husband, but I knew I had to forgive him in order to receive God's forgiveness. I didn't want to hold onto unforgiveness as it was negatively impacting me.

Once I began my healing journey, God started speaking to me through dreams, revealing my purpose and how I had been running away from what He was calling me to do. All I could hear was, "Be still and know that I am God" (Psalm 46:10 NIV) for several months.

I found a counselor to help guide me through the healing process. I began expressing the pain, and she encouraged me to remove the mask, seek true healing, and become the person God has called me to be. I started humbling myself before God, saying, "Lord, I don't know myself. I don't know what real love is. I don't know how to love myself."

I started being vulnerable and transparent, submitting my true feelings to God. I recognized that for years, I had found my identity in the world and through the words spoken over me, allowing my experiences to shape my sense of self. As I began to let go of the false identity, God started revealing my identity in Christ to me. While in His presence, He showed me areas in my marriage where I could have done better.

God revealed to me that I had never dealt with the soul ties I formed in my childhood before getting married. Instead of healing, I had been running away from my problems and holding onto everything I had been through. God showed me how independent I was in my marriage, not allowing my ex-husband to lead. I didn't understand the meaning of submission or how to show respect or honor. In this process, I had to unlearn what I felt unconditional love meant and relearn what love really is.

Unconditional love is not staying in a relationship, tolerating all you can to prove to a person you love them. The Bible defines love in 1 Corinthians 13:4-8, "Love is patient, love is kind. It does not envy, it does not boast, it is not proud. It does not dishonor others, it is not self-seeking, it is not easily angered, it keeps no record of wrongs. Love does not delight in evil but rejoices with the truth. It always protects, always trusts, always hopes, always perseveres. Love never fails" (NIV). As I began to learn the meaning of love and understand that God is love, it helped me love myself and others better.

God showed me myself first and how I used my words to tear down the marriage, instead of building it up. I had been heartbroken for years and made an inner vow that I would never let a man get close to me and break my heart again. I had to revoke all the inner vows I made, even those from my childhood. I had so much anger and aggression built up inside. My heart had become bitter and hardened toward God. But He spoke to me and said that I was receiving a new heart, a heart of flesh, and that He was removing my heart of stone. "I will give you a new heart and put a new spirit in you; I will remove from you your heart of stone and give you a heart of flesh" (Ezekiel 36:26 NIV).

A few months after my divorce was finalized, I committed to celibacy, deciding not to engage in sexual activity until I get married again. One night, while I was sleeping, I woke up with the feeling that I was having sex in my dream. I thought it might be because I was abstaining from sex and it was on my mind, but it continued to happen every time I slept. I started praying, and God revealed to me that I was dealing with a spiritual spouse. Spiritual spouses are demons that visit people in their dreams and engage in sexual acts with them. The demon was speaking in my dreams saying that it had been having sex with me since I was a child. God showed me that the door had been opened through my bloodline due to incest, lust, and the spirit of perversion.

To combat this, I began anointing myself with oil before bed, praying, renouncing unclean spirits, and breaking every covenant made with the spiritual spouse on my behalf and the generations before me. I played prayers and listen to the bible as I slept, it gave me peace. God started revealing generational curses that were affecting my life. I began to see why I dealt with suicidal thoughts and depression, as hard as it was, I knew I couldn't give up.

I found myself constantly engaged in spiritual warfare, but often feeling defeated. God spoke to me and told me that I couldn't fight spiritual battles in the natural realm. I joined a mentoring group and started learning how to engage in spiritual warfare. I had to lift myself up and fight against the Enemy. I had to understand that everything I needed to fight the curses, God has already placed the tools within me. I began to open my mouth and speak against what I was facing. I learned how to decree and declare the Word of God and stand firm on His promises by memorizing, understanding, and meditating on His Word. I also learned the basics of warring in prayer and fasting.

I underwent deliverance sessions with trusted ministries, and over time, I noticed that I was being set free from many things. I began studying and reading books on inner healing, the spirit of rejection, forgiveness, and how to be free from the effects of incest and sexual abuse. I made it a daily practice to sit and read more of God's Word, allowing Him to fill me up and bring me peace. In the midst of my pain, I learned obedience to God. As I released things to the Lord, I found myself growing closer in my relationship with Him. I grew in my walk with God, and He began restoring my identity and bringing healing to my soul. I learned that God can restore what has been lost and broken if we allow Him to work in our lives.

Beloved, I wish above all things that thou mayest prosper and be in health, even as thy soul prospers!

CHAPTER 4

TRANSFORMATION

Do you consider yourself a broken vessel? A broken vessel is a person who feels destroyed, forgotten, flawed, or shattered. Many of us may be broken vessels, but we may not be aware of it because we haven't chosen to revisit the suppressed traumas.

According to Psalm 51:17, 'The sacrifices of God are a broken spirit: a broken and contrite heart, O God, thou wilt not despise.' Similarly, Psalm 34:18 states, 'The Lord is nigh unto them that are of a broken heart and saveth such as be of a contrite spirit'" (KJV). Offering a broken heart to God is a sacrifice that transforms us and influences our thoughts and actions.

Isaiah 64:8 reinforces this idea: "But now, O Lord, thou art our father; we are the clay and thou our potter; and we are all the work of thy hand" (KJV).

When we willingly submit to God's will, He molds, transforms, and sanctifies us as we walk with Him. God knows the purpose for which He called us from our mother's womb, but the Enemy has set up assignments to hinder us. However, we must not allow the trauma and wounds of our souls or the Enemy to deter us. Instead, we must delve deeper into healing and deliverance, striving to walk in wholeness and fulfill God's calling. It's important to understand that healing and deliverance are not one-time events but ongoing processes that require our commitment each day.

The Hebrew word for heal is Rapha (râpâ), which encompasses mending, curing, repairing, making whole, and acting as a physician (Jehovah Rapha – the God that heals). Deliverance, on the other hand, refers to the act of liberating, rescuing, and setting someone free. As Christians, we require both healing and deliverance to experience transformation. Inner healing and deliverance provide us with the ability to draw closer to God.

Now, let's discuss trauma. Trauma is defined as an event, series of events, or set of circumstances that an individual experiences as physically or emotionally harmful or threatening, with lasting adverse effects on their functioning and physical, social, and emotional well-being. Trauma can occur at any point in life, but it is most likely during childhood when we encounter various types of traumatic experiences.

Children can be affected by the sins of their parents and previous generations. Some childhood trauma may be the result of generational curses, which involve curses passed down through the family based on the sins, misdeeds, or actions of relatives (both deceased and living).

Exodus 34:7 supports the existence of generational curses: "Keeping mercy for thousands, forgiving iniquity and transgression and sin, and that will by no means clear the guilty; visiting the iniquity of the fathers upon the children, and upon the children's children, unto the third and to the fourth generation" (KJV). Although we were innocent during childhood, we are not exempt from the effects of generational curses.

Secrets kept within the family can keep you in agreement with curses. Ask God which generational curses are affecting your life. To be free from these curses, you must confess the sins and repent on behalf of your parents and the preceding generations. Denounce your agreement with the curse and choose to walk away from those sins.

Everyone responds to trauma differently. What is your response when you face trauma? Do you suppress it and shut down? Do you turn to God? Do you seek help from wise counsel? Or do you repay evil with evil? Your primary response should be to turn to God. He knows exactly what you're facing, and He is willing to heal your broken heart and bind up your wounds.

Experiencing trauma in your life does not mean you have to live in brokenness and despair. Often, we allow trauma to take root and fester. Holding onto trauma opens the doors for other negative influences to enter your life and can even cause physical health problems. Trauma leads us to build walls and live in fear, resentment, and unforgiveness as a means to protect ourselves from further pain. However, it is crucial to seek healing from trauma. Your wounds do not define you or your future.

When we allow our wounds to define us and label ourselves based on our experiences, we develop a false identity. False identity refers to an incorrect understanding or perception of who we are. Placing your identity in unstable or inconsistent things will always leave you searching for your true self. Once you are saved, you become a new creation in God's image. The verse from 2 Corinthians 5:17 affirms this: "Therefore if any man be in Christ, he is a new creature: old things are passed away; behold, all things are become new" (KJV).

Your identity can only be found in Christ, not in zodiac signs, horoscopes, people, or any other sources. Remove the labels that were placed on you by experiences, people, or the world. Believe what God says about you, not what others say. Let go of your false identity and embrace your true identity in Christ.

When you experience healing and walk in your God-given identity, you become a weapon of God. There is true power in accepting and walking as the person God has called you to be.

Who the Son sets free is free indeed!

CHAPTER 5

FREEDOM

*A*re you ready to start the process of healing? Each person's journey of healing and deliverance will be unique. During the process of transformation, numerous changes will occur within us and through us. I was once bound by brokenness until I decided to partner with God and begin my journey toward healing and wholeness. As I have submitted who I am and my character to God, I have witnessed many changes.

God has taught me various ways to value and love myself, emphasizing the importance of being gentle and granting me the grace to grow. I have learned to prioritize myself and avoid depleting my energy by constantly trying to please others. While my brokenness was once a stumbling block, I can now serve and assist others in areas where I have experienced healing. I no longer respond to triggers and people who wrong me in the same way. God has shown me how to be vulnerable and communicate in healthy ways, enabling me to foster lasting and healthy relationships with others.

God has genuinely transformed my life, granting me freedom in various areas. The extent of our freedom is determined by the extent to which we allow God to reign freely over every aspect of our lives. Seeking God's guidance and allowing the Holy Spirit to lead us should always be our first priority in attaining freedom. I would like to share some basic steps of healing and deliverance that the Lord has placed on my heart to assist you in your own process of transformation.

STEPS TO HEALING

- **Surrender**
  Repent. Release hurt and pain to God. "Casting all your care upon him, for he careth for you" (1 Peter 5:7 KJV).

- **Search Your Heart**
  Ask God to search your heart so that He can bring forth the things that you

suppressed and allow you to get to the root of the pain.

"Search me, O God, and know my heart: try me and know my thoughts" (Psalm 139:23 KJV).

- **Forgive**
Forgive others so that you may be forgiven. It doesn't mean that what was done to you was right, but God is the only One who can repay. Take time to forgive God, yourself, and others.

"For if ye forgive men their trespasses, your heavenly Father will also forgive you" (Matthew 6:14 KJV).

- **Pray**
Keep yourself covered in prayer every day. Prayer will help bring forth healing in your life. Never stop praying. Even if you feel you got a breakthrough in healing, keep interceding!

"Pray without ceasing" (1 Thessalonians 5:17 KJV).

- **Be Accountable**
  Recognize and accept the mistakes that you have made throughout your life. Don't dwell on your mistakes, learn from them. You may have to call someone and ask for forgiveness, but this is a necessary step in healing. Find other believers of Christ, wise counsel, and ask them to keep you covered in prayer for healing. Wise counsel will hold you accountable for healing and be able to perceive what you can't see such as blind spots or weaknesses. I also recommend finding a therapist to partner with you as you go through your journey.

  "Iron sharpeneth iron; So a man sharpeneth the countenance of his friend" (Proverbs 27:17 KJV).

- **Read the Word of God**
  Feed your faith. Take time to read the Word of God daily. Study scriptures on healing your heart. If the Holy Spirit prompts you, you can read other books on inner healing. Believe

that you're healed, even before you actually see the results.

"So then faith cometh by hearing and hearing by the word of God" (Romans 10:17 KJV).

- **Guard Your Heart**
Allow the Lord to protect your heart through His Word. Avoid holding on to grudges and be quick to forgive. Don't allow your emotions to lead you. Bring your emotions to God and let Him lead you. Be intentional about what you're thinking. Reject what is not true and the lies from the Enemy. Speak declarations and the truth over yourself daily.

"Keep thy heart with all diligence; for out of it are the issues of life" (Proverbs 4:23 KJV).

STEPS TO DELIVERANCE

- **Repent**
  Confess your sins and turn away from them. True repentance requires you to change your ways. Seek the Lord and ask what changes need to be made.

  "Repent ye therefore, and be converted, that your sins may be blotted out, when the times of refreshing shall come from the presence of the Lord" (Acts 3:19 KJV).

- **Get Rooted in Christ**
  Ask God to lead you to a church home. Get to know Him by reading His Word and praying. Develop a walk of dependency on God. Allow Him into your everyday decision-making.

  "As ye have therefore received Christ Jesus the Lord, so walk ye in him. Rooted and built up in him, and established in the faith, as ye have been taught, abounding therein with thanksgiving" (Colossians 2:6-7 KJV).

- **Forgive**
  Forgive others so that you may be forgiven. It doesn't mean that what was done to you was right, but God is the only One who can repay. Take time to forgive God, yourself, and others.

  "For if ye forgive men their trespasses, your heavenly Father will also forgive you" (Matthew 6:14 KJV).

- **Fast and Pray**
  Some issues that we deal with are not defeated except through fasting and praying. Fasting and praying can restore and strengthen your intimacy with God. Fasting creates discipline in your life and helps you bring your flesh under subjection. If you have never fasted before, read scriptures about fasting, pray, and ask God to provide instructions on how you should fast and when to do so. Fasting should be a part of your journey with God.

Freedom

In Matthew 17:21 it is written: "Howbeit this kind goeth not out but by prayer and fasting" (KJV).

- **Be Set Free**
  God wants you to experience freedom. It is important to involve a deliverance minister in this step, especially if it is your first time going through deliverance. I do not recommend attempting it alone. Find a Holy Spirit-filled deliverance minister or ministry that can guide you through the process. In this step, you will need to renounce strongholds, break curses, and may even require the casting out of spirits. If you are uncertain about what you are dealing with, seek guidance from God. Remember that each person's journey of deliverance will be different.

As stated in John 8:36 "If the Son therefore shall make you free, ye shall be free indeed" (KJV).

- **Fill Yourself with God's Word**
  After experiencing deliverance and being set free, it is important to immerse ourselves in the Word of

God to counter the spirit that has been cast out. For instance, if you were struggling with doubt and unbelief, you should saturate yourself with scriptures about faith, trust, and so on. Building our lives on God's Word should be a daily practice. We need to fill ourselves with the Word to effectively combat the Enemy. It is not enough to simply read the Word; we must study and meditate on it. God's words are filled with spirit and life. If we choose to apply them to our daily lives, they can bring about life-changing transformations.

There are various ways to fill ourselves with more of the Word. Some examples include writing down and memorizing scriptures, composing declarations, listening to the audio Bible, and engaging with teachings that are filled with the Word of God. It is the truth of God's Word that will set us free.

As stated in Joshua 1:8, "This book of the law shall not depart out of thy mouth; but thou shalt meditate therein day and night, that thou mayest observe to do according to all that is written therein: for then thou shalt make thy way prosperous, and then thou shalt have good success" (KJV).

- **Resist the Enemy**
  Avoid old habits that can lead you to sin and backsliding. Reject the lies of the Enemy. Be quick to tear down anything that is not of God. Learn to clothe yourself in the whole armor of God every day so that you can stand against the Enemy's tricks. Guard your ears and eyes, and stay vigilant against any temptations the Enemy may bring. Be cautious about the company you keep and fix your focus on the Lord. Commit to walking in righteousness and renew your mind daily.

  "Submit yourselves therefore to God. Resist the devil, and he will flee from you" (James 4:7 KJV).

- **Worship and Praise**
  Worship and praise are powerful tools that we can utilize in our journey with God. Through worship, captives can

be set free, evil spirits can be driven out, and strongholds can be broken. We can express our worship through music, dancing, soaking, and spending time in God's presence. It is important to maintain a reverent attitude toward God and walk with a heart of thanksgiving. Continually praise God for who He is and for the trials He has brought you through. Remember that God eagerly awaits us in our times of worship and praise.

As you embark on your healing journey, there are important things to remind yourself of. Throughout your own journey of healing and deliverance, God will provide you with revelations. Always remember that you are never alone; God is with you during times of pain. "Be strong and courageous. Do not be afraid or terrified because of them, for the LORD your God goes with you; he will never leave you nor forsake you" (Deuteronomy 31:6 KJV).

- **Make Peace with Your Journey**
  While I may not know the specifics of your past, it is crucial to make peace

with it to move forward. Even if you struggle during the healing process, remember that you are not a failure. Get back up and start over; the goal is to never give up. I encourage you to celebrate the milestones you achieve along the way as the healing journey can be challenging. Healing and deliverance are ongoing processes throughout our lives. Only Jehovah God can heal and set you free. Only the one true and living God possesses that power. Time alone does not heal wounds; you must actively seek and receive your healing.

You deserve healing. So, today, choose to let go of brokenness and take steps toward transformation and wholeness. God is the ultimate physician, so allow Him to transform you from the inside out.

Healing and wholeness are your portions, child of God! Declare: "God is healing my heart and making me whole! In Jesus' name!"

AFFIRMATIONS

IDENTITY IN CHRIST

I am a child of God.

"Dear friends, now we are children of God, and what we will be has not yet been made known. But we know that when Christ appears, we shall be like him, for we shall see him as he is" (1 John 3:2 NIV).

I am healed.

"He himself bore our sins in his body on the cross, so that we might die to sins and live for righteousness; by his wounds, you have been healed" (1 Peter 2:24 NIV).

I am loved.

"As the Father has loved me, so have I loved you. Now remain in my love" (John 15:9 NIV).

I am free.

"If the Son therefore shall make you free, ye shall be free indeed" (John 8:36 KJV).

I am a new creature.

"Therefore if any man be in Christ, he is a new creature: old things are passed away; behold, all things are become new" (2 Corinthians 5:17 KJV).

I am forgiven.

"Therefore, my friends, I want you to know that through Jesus the forgiveness of sins is proclaimed to you. 'Through him everyone who believes is set free from every sin, a justification you were not able to obtain under the law of Moses" (Acts 13:38-39 NIV).

I am qualified.

"Not that we are sufficiently qualified in ourselves to claim anything as *coming* from us, but our sufficiency *and* qualifications come from God" (2 Corinthians 3:5 AMP).

I am strong.

"Finally, be strong in the Lord and in his mighty power" (Ephesians 6:10 NIV).

I am accepted.

"To the praise of the glory of his grace, wherein he hath made us accepted in the beloved" (Ephesians 1:6 KJV).

I am complete in Christ.

"So you are complete through your union with Christ, who is the head over every ruler and authority" (Colossians 2:10 NLT).

I am God's masterpiece.

"For we are God's masterpiece. He has created us anew in Christ Jesus, so we can do the good things he planned for us long ago" (Ephesians 2:10 NLT).

I am blessed.

"Blessed be the God and Father of our Lord Jesus Christ, who hath blessed us with all Spiritual blessings in heavenly places in Christ" (Ephesians 1:3 KJV).

I am uniquely gifted.

"Just as each one of you has received a *special* gift [a spiritual talent, an ability graciously given by God], employ it in serving one another as [is appropriate for] good stewards of God's multifaceted grace [faithfully using the diverse, varied gifts and abilities granted to Christians by God's unmerited favor]" (1 Peter 4:10 AMP).

I have purpose.

"'For I know the plans I have for you,' declares the Lord, 'plans to prosper you and not harm you, plans to give you hope and a future'" (Jeremiah 29:11 NIV).

I am redeemed.

"I have blotted out, as a thick cloud, thy transgressions, and as a cloud, thy sins: return unto me; for I have redeemed thee" (Isaiah 44:22 KJV).

EXERCISES

Create your own affirmations. Write down some affirmations that you can use daily to speak over yourself and encourage yourself.

Exercise

Forgiveness

"Bearing with one another and, if one has a complaint against another, forgiving each other; as the Lord has forgiven you, so you also must forgive" (Colossians 3:13 ESV).

Search your heart today. What do you need to forgive yourself for? Ask God to show you whom you need to forgive. Repent, and ask Him to help you to forgive the individual(s)

Journal your answers and thoughts:

Healed, Whole, and Dangerous to the Kingdom of Hell

Exercises

Exercise

Unhealed Trauma

"He heals the brokenhearted and binds up their wounds" (Psalm 147:3).

Sit before God and let Him reveal things that you need to heal from. What happened in your childhood that you haven't healed from? What's the one thing you can't tell anyone, but it still hurts you to this day? Begin your healing process today! Release the pain and ask God to heal you!

Journal your answers and thoughts.

_____
_____
_____
_____
_____
_____
_____
_____
_____

Exercises

Healed, Whole, and Dangerous to the Kingdom of Hell

Exercise

Identity in Christ

"So God created mankind in his own image, in the image of God he created them; male and female he created them" (Genesis 1:27).

Who does God say you are? You were created in God's image. He knows you and who you are created to be! Pray and ask Him to reveal who you are. What's your purpose?

Journal your answers and thoughts.

Healed, Whole, and Dangerous to the Kingdom of Hell

PRAYERS

Salvation Prayer

Lord, I repent and ask for forgiveness of my sins. I believe that Jesus died on the cross for my sins and rose from the dead three days later. I confess Jesus as my Lord and Savior. Lord, come into my heart and take complete control of my life. Lord, fill me with Your Holy Spirit and help me to do Your will. Thank You, Lord, for saving me. In Jesus' name. Amen.

Healing from Sexual Abuse Prayer

Dear Heavenly Father, I confess the sin of incest and sexual abuse for myself and my bloodline. I come out of agreement with any family secrets and generational curses of incest, rape, and molestation. Father, I forgive myself and the person(s) who raped or molested me. I forgive those whom I felt should have protected and saved me from being raped and molested.

I command any ungodly soul tie that was created by sexual abuse to be severed and burned! In the mighty name of Jesus. I cast down and destroy every spirit of shame that I allowed to enter my soul because I was sexually abused. Despite what I have been through, I declare that I am fearfully and wonderfully made. I shut down memory recall that causes me to play the sexual acts in my mind over and over. I decree that my mind is washed and renewed today! In Jesus' name.

I drive out distrust that causes me not to trust people. I declare that I can trust and have healthy, whole relationships. I command all doors that were open to lust and perversion through incest, rape, and molestation to be closed now! In Jesus' name. I dismantle the fear of my children going through sexual abuse. Lord, I give my children to You and allow You to lead and protect them. Father, Your Word says to cast my burdens on You, Lord, and You will sustain me.

Father, I give You the burden that comes behind incest, rape, and molestation. Lord, I surrender the hurt that came into my life from sexual abuse. I plead the blood of Jesus over my heart, mind, and emotions. I unleash supernatural healing over myself. Lord, I thank You for healing me and setting me free from sexual abuse. In Jesus' name. I bind all backlash and retaliation, and I seal this prayer in the blood of Jesus. Amen.

Emotional Healing and Wholeness Prayer

Father, in the name of Jesus, I ask You to come into my heart and heal me from emotional wounds and childhood trauma. Lord, I give You my heart and allow You to perform supernatural heart surgery. Lord, You have permission to remove anything that's not like You.

Father, go deep into my heart and uproot the pain and wounds that I suppressed over the years. Lord, Your Word says that You are near to the broken-hearted and You save those with a crushed spirit. Release healing and restore where my spirit has been crushed. I shut down childhood trauma so it will not hinder my healing and progress. I call on You, Jehovah Rapha, the God that heals.

Heal my broken heart and bind up my wounds. In the name of Jesus. I lay down my hardened, stony heart, and I pick up Your heart, Lord, a heart of flesh. I take authority over suicidal thoughts and depression, and I command them to go. God, You came that I may have life and have it abundantly. I declare that I will never be depressed again. I tear down every spirit of heaviness in my life and put on a garment of praise. Thank You, Father, forgive me and give me beauty for ashes. I cast out rejection and declare that I am loved and accepted by the beloved. Lord, deliver me from tormenting spirits, fear, sickness, deep hurt, guilt, loneliness, hatred, confusion, resentment, offense, stress, anger, sorrow, anxiety, grief, and oppression.

Many are the afflictions of the righteous, but I thank You, Lord, for delivering me from all my afflictions. Lord, purify my heart and teach me how to guard my heart and mind. I release the fruits of the Spirit into my life: love, joy, peace, patience, kindness, goodness, faithfulness, gentleness, and self-control. I praise You, Lord, for making my heart new. I trust You, Lord, and I rely on You for complete healing and wholeness. In Jesus' name, I bind all backlash and retaliation, and I seal this prayer in the blood of Jesus. Amen.

Walking in Purpose and Christ's Identity Prayer

Father, in the name of Jesus, I come to You asking that You reveal to me why I was created. Lord, Your Word says You formed my inward parts and knitted me together in my mother's womb. You knew me before I was born. Lord, show me Your perfect will for my life. It is written that Your ways are higher than my ways and Your plans are greater than mine. I surrender and commit myself to God's plan for my life.

Father, I command my heart to be aligned with Yours, my ideas to be aligned with Yours, and my will to be aligned with Yours. Father, I repent for trying to find identity in any source other than You, Lord. I reject and denounce all false identities that I may have found in witchcraft, horoscopes, and zodiac signs. I break off and destroy every word curse that alters my identity, and I declare all word curses spoken over my life to be null and void. In Jesus' name, I decree that I am a child of God, a friend of God, and that I belong to You, Father.

Lord, today, I strip off false identities and remove the mask that prevents me from seeing who I am in You. Help me to see myself as You see me, Lord. I pray that the eyes of my understanding be enlightened so that I may know the hope of my calling. I declare that I have a purpose because I was chosen by God from the foundation of the world.

I set ablaze anything that will hinder me from seeing my purpose, and I cancel any assignment that will try to prevent me from walking in my God-given identity. Lord, release supernatural confidence upon me to boldly walk in my purpose and strengthen me to be a warrior for the kingdom of God. In Jesus' name, I bind all backlash and retaliation, and I seal this prayer in the blood of Jesus. Amen.

Unforgiveness Prayer

Dear Heavenly Father, I repent of holding onto unforgiveness in my heart. Today, I give You my burden of unforgiveness and ask for Your help in forgiving those who have hurt, wounded, offended, and mistreated me. Lord, Your Word says that I must first forgive anyone I am holding a grudge against so that my Father in heaven may forgive my sins as well. Lord, if there is any hidden resentment in my heart toward You, God, please expose it so that I may confess it and be forgiven. Lord, I forgive myself for any past mistakes.

Father, I forgive every person and every situation that I have held onto in my mind and heart. (Call out names/events that need to be forgiven) Help me to see those who have hurt me through Your eyes so that I may love them as You love them. I choose to let go of any bitterness, anger, and wrath that came in through unforgiveness, and I command every door that was opened through unforgiveness to be closed now! In Jesus' name. Lord, help me to forgive seventy times seven. I pray that if I have offended anyone, Lord, that You would bring it to my mind so that I may seek forgiveness. Thank You, Lord, for setting me free from unforgiveness and bitterness. In Jesus' name. I bind all backlash and retaliation, and I seal this prayer in the blood of Jesus. Amen.

Resources

If you or someone you know has been sexually assaulted, abused, or suicidal, help is available.

Sexual Assault and Harassment

National Sexual Assault Hotline: a service of RAINN

Telephone hotline: 800-656-4673

Telephone hotline: 866-811-7473

Domestic and Dating Violence

National Domestic Violence Hotline

Telephone hotline: 800-799-7233

Telephone hotline: 866-331-9474

Suicide

National Suicide Prevention Lifeline

Telephone Hotline: 988 (call or text)

Telephone Hotline: 800-273-8255

Other Resources & Tips:

- Seek deliverance through a trusted ministry.
- Find a therapist or counselor.
- If you are a teen or young adult, I encourage you to talk to your parents and have conversations about what you're experiencing or may have experienced.

Bibliography

Strong, James. Strong's Exhaustive Concordance Of The Bible. Hendrickson Publishers, 2007.

Brodie, Jessica. "Are Generational Curses Real Today?" Crosswalk.com, Crosswalk.com, 6 Oct. 2020, https://www.crosswalk.com/faith/bible-study/are-generational-curses-real-today.html.

Bratcher, Dennis. "Broken Vessel." Wiktionary, 16 Oct. 2022, https://en.wiktionary.org/wiki/broken vessel.

"Deliverance Definition & Meaning." Merriam-Webster, Merriam-Webster, https://www.merriam-webster.com/dictionary/deliverance.

"Trauma-Informed Care." Trauma-Informed Care | Early Connections, https://earlyconnections.mo.gov/professionals/trauma-informed-care.

Powell, Aubrie. "Inner Vows." The ANCHOR Church, The ANCHOR Church, 24 Feb. 2019, https://theanchor.me/sermon-notes/2019/2/24/2019-02-24-inner-vows-sermon.

About the Author

Nykia White was born in Saint Louis, Missouri. She is the third of five siblings. Nykia was raised to fear God and love others. Prior to pursuing ministry, she worked in healthcare for ten years. She is a new entrepreneur and the founder of Purposeful Scents. Nykia has a passion for helping people and loves engaging in community outreach. She currently resides in Atlanta, Georgia. To stay connected with Nykia, you can follow her on various social media platforms.

Connect with Nykia

Instagram: Kiaakiaa314

YouTube: PurposedbyAbba

Website: PurposedbyAbba.com

Email: PurposedbyAbba@gmail.com

Made in the USA
Columbia, SC
17 September 2023